Instagram Like a Boss!

Insider Secrets to Boost your Personal & Business Brand

A Quick Guide by

Mo Said | Grow Social Flow

Ready to Boss Up your Instagram Game? Let's Go!

Ever scratch your head wondering how those short vids and awesome pics can actually boost your business on Instagram? Well, it's not rocket science and luckily you don't need a PhD in Social Media Marketing to master this platform. Instagram's been the secret sauce for personal and business brands to connect with their customers in more ways than one. So, how can you join the Instagram bandwagon for your business? Here's a handy guide with some cool tools and not-so-secret secret strategies to help you hit the Instagram jackpot- Cha-CHING!

So, you're done playing around on Instagram and FINALLY Ready to Get Down to Business?

Instagram, it's not just for brunch pics and dog selfies anymore. Shocking, right? Businesses are sliding into those DMs, and Instagram is here for it. They've even rolled out the red carpet with their Instagram for Business Blog. It's jam-packed with tips, tricks, and the 411 on how to turn that fun little app into a business-boosting powerhouse. So, are you ready to take your Insta game from lit to legit to too damn big to quit?

Whether or not you're fresh on the 'gram and looking to shake things up with your biz, first things first, get your head in the Instagram for Business Blog. It's the motherlode of tips, tricks, and insta-wisdom straight from the horse's mouth. Think of it as Instagram 101 for business buffs. Why waste time guessing when you can get the lowdown straight from HQ? Be smart. Be savvy. Start your insta-journey with the Instagram for Business Blog.

Here's the link: https://business.instagram.com/

You're welcome!

The Fine Art of Promoting Your Personal or Business Brand

Believe it or not, Instagram is more than just a platform for sharing trending quotes and viral cat videos (I mean, who doesn't love those). While it's perfect for casual scrolling, it's also a goldmine for savvy entrepreneurs looking to boost their businesses. Yes, that snapshot of avocado toast could lead you to your next big opportunity. Remember, it's not all about food pics and daily outfit posts. Striking a balance between captivating content and promotional messages is key. Experiment with it and watch your business shine amid latte art and beach scenes.

Looking to level up your Instagram with fun pics? Cool, cool. But hey, don't turn your feed into a meme page. Got a business to promote? Then make sure to throw in some promotional images and videos too. Keep your audience clued in. Show them you're more than just a good time - you mean business. Balance, my friend, that's the key. A sprinkle of fun, a dash of business - that's your recipe for Insta-success. Got it? Good. Now, go forth and conquer that feed.

The No-Brainer Science of Building your Instagram Followers

Are you looking to be Insta-famous? Well, you're gonna need followers, and lots of 'em. See, your Instagram game is only as strong as your follower count. More followers equals more chances to hustle your brand on the 'gram. And let's be real, who doesn't want a bigger piece of that Insta-pie? Lucky for you, there's a bunch of surefire ways to stack up those followers. So get ready, 'cause you're about to become a big deal on Instagram. Trust me, it'll be epic.

Tip number 1: link your Instagram account with your Facebook. That's correct! Instagram offers a cool feature allowing you to connect it to your Facebook, like a two-for-one social media deal. Post a selfie on Instagram, and voilà! It appears on your Facebook as well. And who owns both platforms? Yes, you're right, the same tech giant. It's akin to having a double-decker social media treat. By connecting your accounts, you can reach both your Facebook friends and Instagram followers simultaneously. So, go on and link those profiles. You'll soon be flooded with likes and shares. Who says you can't have the best of both worlds?

Tip number 2: cross-post a few chosen pics and clips right onto your Facebook page. Align them with your Insta campaign and boom - your Facebook folks will know you're rockin' it on Instagram too. Isn't it time your Facebook audience got in on the action?

It's like killing two birds with one photo, right? Especially when you're the new kid on the Instagram block and you're trying to get your Facebook fam to notice. So, why not align your Insta campaigns with your Facebook posts? Not only will you grow your Insta gang, but, hey, your business might just get the boost it needs. How's that for a twofer?

Tip number 3: looking to make an even bigger splash on Instagram? Here's the scoop. To become an Instagram sensation, riding the hashtag wave is key. These "#" symbols serve as entrances to the realm of viral content magic. Social media enthusiasts flock to trending tags like magnets, hungry for the latest updates, exciting rumors, and fresh memes. By blending your promotional posts with these popular hashtags, you can swiftly connect with a wider audience. With skill, you might even find yourself mingling with top influencers in the digital realm. Just keep in mind, this isn't a game of chance. Success requires strategy, smarts, and determination. Are you up for the challenge?

Tip number 4: if you really wanna fire up your Instagram game, then do this: mix it up with the Insta-celebs aka Influencers, throw some likes on their posts. You scratch their back, they'll scratch yours - it's the unwritten Insta law, after all. Start a like-for-like trend and watch your posts become hotter than a summer's day. It's a tried and tested method - no magic tricks, just good old reciprocation. Trust us, it works if you work it, so get liking and commenting!

Get Shooting! Boss Up with Reels

So, you see yourself as an Instagram influencer, eh? Well, allow me to share some insights. Jump on the reels trend, my friend. But not just any videos – create eye-catching content that offers a glimpse into your world, leaving your followers intrigued.

Remember when X (fka Twitter) dominated the video scene with Vine? Instagram stepped up with a challenge: "Watch this!" With 90 seconds of customizable video content, Instagram is giving Vine's 6.5 seconds a run for its money.

Why should this matter to you? It's simple. Trending reels attract followers like catnip. More videos mean more followers and increased business promotion. So, why hesitate? Get filming now!

Cheat Code: Embed Reels on your Site!

Hey, remember when Instagram was all "Nah, you can't have a desktop version, you get what you get and you don't get upset?" Well, they finally pulled their heads out of the sand and gave the people what they wanted. What's new, you ask? An embed feature, my friend. Yep, you can now plaster your short videos all over your website or blog like a proud parent with a fridge full of kindergartener art. Why, you ask? Well, who knows how many eyeballs actually land on your posts in the social media abyss? Embed those vids, and boom - you just multiplied your chances of hitting the viewer jackpot. Now go forth and conquer, you social media maven, you.

So, you've got these fire Instagram videos and a website that's begging for more traffic. What now? Well, how about killing two birds with one stone? Give your website visitors a taste of your Instagram magic. It's like giving them a backstage pass to your brand. And guess what? They'll probably love it so much, they'll head right over to your Instagram and hit follow. More followers, more visibility. Boom! Instagram's shiny embed feature lets you share your vids on your site. It's like inviting your website visitors over to your Instagram party. So why not? Get on it!

Be a Following Leader and a Leading Follower!

Ever wondered why your Insta game isn't as strong as it could be? Maybe you're just not playing it right. You see, some businesses, especially those big hot-shot accounts, have a bad habit. They rack up followers but don't follow 'em back. No give and take, no real connection. Yeah, they've got the numbers, but what about loyalty?

Here's the real kicker: to truly win at Instagram, flip the script. Follow your followers back. Sounds simple, right? It's a game-changer. It's like saying, "Hey, I see you. You matter." And who doesn't want to feel seen? It's not just about racking up followers; it's about building a legit community where your followers feel valued.

Ready to seriously step up your Insta game? Start hitting that follow-back button. Guaranteed, it's a solid move for boosting your brand. Your move, champ.

Boss Up Your Content Calendar!

Hey, everyone's got an Insta-game plan these days. But let's get real, you're not gonna win followers by bombarding them with a million posts a day. It's not a sprint, it's a marathon. You've gotta strategically drip-feed them that sweet, sweet content. Give 'em a chance to miss you a little, yeah? And remember, no one likes that friend who won't stop talking about themselves. Don't be that friend. You've gotta give your followers a moment to breathe, to digest that killer content you're serving up. Uploading too much, too fast? That's a one-way ticket to Unfollowville, my friend. Keep it chill, keep it fresh. You've got this.

Hey, ever had that "Oops, I did it again" moment? You know, when you've accidentally posted the same cat meme twice on your Instagram? Yeah, it's a bit of a facepalm moment. A content calendar can save you from these blushes. Plus, it gives you a bird's eye view of what's hitting the mark and what's sinking like a lead balloon. Some posts are like catnip to your audience, others... not so much. So, let's get it together, folks! A killer content calendar is your secret sauce to keep your Insta game strong. Remember, it's not just about throwing spaghetti at the wall and seeing what sticks. It's about serving up the good stuff that keeps your followers coming back for more. When you know what works and what doesn't, you'll spend less time figuring out what to post and when to post it, and more time posting what hits the mark at the right days and times. You'll thank us later and you'll be glad you did! Remember, consistency is key.

The Sacred Golden Rule: Stay On Brand!

Major tip incoming! Write these three simple words somewhere, plaster it on a wall or on your fridge or on your mirror: Stay On Brand! Meaning, post quality content relevant to your brand/image. Being relevant (and consistent) at all times makes you look professional. It is always important to post images and short videos that are relevant to your brand. Identify your brand's color palette, fonts, style of writing. And stick to it with every single post, caption, image and video you upload and share. When this is done correctly, you stand a chance of making your Instagram page even more identifiable with your brand and stand out from the crowd. On most occasions, businesses on Instagram make irrelevant posts that have nothing to do with their brand. In doing so, they confuse their audiences. This is an implication that they do not offer their audience a definite line of identification. If you don't know who you are or what your brand is, don't expect your followers to either!

To become an Insta-star, it takes time, focus and lots of work. Step one: Stop posting random junk. People on the Internet have the attention span of a goldfish. If you're not relevant, you're invisible. And consistency? That's your new best friend. No one cares about your once-in-a-blue-moon "inspirational" quote. Deliver the goods, regularly and you might just stand a chance in the mad, mad world of social media.

Boost your Instagram Page Engagement with a Contest or Free Giveaways!

Remember, in the Insta-arena, it's survival of the fittest (or should we say, the most consistent and relevant?). So, are you game? Rhetorical question: you know you are, that's why you got this badass book!

Who needs a megaphone when you've got giveaways? Dangle a freebie or a contest in front of your followers and watch them scramble. Have them tag, mention, share, and basically shout your name from the digital rooftops. It's like having your own personal army of brand ambassadors. It's a deliciously sneaky way to grow your Instagram tribe. Who said there's no such thing as a free lunch?

Tip incoming! Looking to score a perfect ten with your Instagram contest or giveaways? Pick a theme that's not just fun & catchy (i.e. relatable and relevant to your brand), but also a sweet deal for your audience (something that gets them excited to participate and pass on the word). Make sure it's got a bit of your brand's spirit in it too (sprinkle some of your own fairy dust on it). Once you've got that down, slap that contest on your Insta and hitch it to your Facebook for some extra lovin' love. Play your cards right and watch the likes roll in. Not only will your followers be buzzing, they'll be bringing their friends into the mix too. Who said selling out couldn't be fun, right?

Another tip incoming! Wanna make your contest, or giveaways go crazy viral on Instagram? Hashtags, my friend, are your secret weapon. Organize your contest with killer hashtags and watch your audience just explode (figuratively speaking of course). Okay, let's keep it real here. Sometimes, it can spread like wildfire, and you'll have tens, then hundreds of new followers and likes and shares. And other times, it might be a very slow drip like a leaky tweaky faucet. Just don't get discouraged, and keep trying different themes, use different strategies and tactics. Trial and error, till you finally hit bullseye- remember, consistency is key. Don't give up!

Real world example: Samsung Camera. They used the hashtag #LiveInTheMoment to promote their photo contest, which was also linked to their Facebook page. And guess what? It worked! The hashtag drew people in and caught like lightning. Who knew 15 characters could be so powerful? So, when it comes to promoting your contest or giveaways on Instagram, don't forget the power of the mighty hashtag. It might just be the social media marketing tool you didn't know you needed. Now go forth, and practice what you just learned.

Ride the Trending Wave

Social media, right? Suddenly, we've all got the world at our fingertips. News travels faster than the speed of gossip in a small town. Got a phone and a social media account? Boom, you're in the know. And not just about Aunt Susan's cat's birthday party. We're talking real, important stuff here. The latest trends? They're blowing up on your feed before you can say "viral." And let's be honest, we all love being the first to know, don't we? It's like we're all mini news reporters, sharing the scoop and raking in those sweet, sweet likes. Talk about a power trip!

Trending on social media? More like free advertising! Sure, not every hot topic will fit your brand, but with a little creativity, you can spin that buzz into gold. Be selective. Don't just jump on any trending bandwagon. Always ask yourself: Is this on brand with my brand? You'll get to a certain point where you'll be so good at picking and choosing the trending, you'll eventually start your own trend! Till then, it's a lot like a game of *connect the dots* between what's trending and your brand's message and identity. Nail it and watch your Instagram followers multiply like rabbits. Who knew riding the wave of trends could be your secret weapon to smashing those promo goals?

Boss Up your Inta-Networking Skills!

Instagram, not just the virtual land of selfies and foodies. There's more to it. It's a goldmine for business promotion, but you gotta play the game, and play it right. It's more than just posing, taking selfies and uploading with a fire caption. The secret that no one talks about is this: Instagram is all about connecting, and making the right types of connections is key. It's like a giant web of movers and shakers, and you've got to get tangled up in it (minus the drama of course, always keep it classy and professional). How? Well, ever thought about simply liking and commenting on other folks' posts? It's not rocket science, but it works. And hashtags? More like cash-tags, am I right? Engage, interact, and watch your network grow like social flow. Stop being shy, get out there and start networking like a Boss! You might just be surprised at what you can achieve with a few well-timed likes, comments and hashtags.

Treat Loyalty Like Royalty

Instagram, that magical land where likes and shares are the currency. But what about those MVPs who always double-tap your posts? They deserve a little sumthin' sumthin', don't they? And no, I'm not talking about a virtual pat on the back. Treat loyalty like royalty. Rewarding your most loyal legion of die-hard followers isn't just a nice thing to do, it's also a smart move to keep 'em coming back for more. They're your brand's biggest ambassadors. If Instagram is the hive, you're the Queen Bee, and they're your army of bees pollinating and cultivating that sweet sweet honey (the nectar of likes, comments, mentions and shares!) But what incentives to offer them in return? Well, that's the million-dollar question, isn't it? Just remember, keep it relevant, on-brand, and for goodness sake, don't promote your competitors – that's just free advertising for them, and who needs that?

Now let's talk incentivization aka treats. Yeah, you heard me, treats! You know, those sweet little extras that get your followers buzzing like bees to honey. I'm talking about VIP passes, promo codes, the works. But let's be real, these incentives aren't one-size-fits-all. What works for fashion brands might not cut it for your homemade candle business. So, make sure your treats align with your brand. What was that Sacred Golden Rule again? If you forgot it already, go back and read that short chapter over and over till it sinks in.

Listen, it's not all sunshine and rainbows. Don't toss around freebies like you're Santa on Christmas morning. Keep 'em hooked, make 'em refresh your feed more than their inbox. But remember, less is more. You don't want to be that guy or gal at the party, broke from buying rounds for everyone, right?

FYI: Insta-fame doesn't have a price tag. So don't go nuts handing out free stuff until you're broke and regretting life decisions. Keep it chill, keep it light, and remember, a little goes a long way on the 'Gram. Capisce? Good!

Sneak Peaks and BTS (Behind-The-Scenes) to Generate Buzz

Posting pics of your finished products on Insta is getting kind of stale, don't you think? Your followers are practically begging for a fresh take. How about serving up some behind-the-scenes realness? Show them the nitty gritty - the production hustle, the management bustle, the art of packaging. It's like taking the road less traveled, but with more likes. Why blend in when you can stand out? Wave goodbye to the usual, and say hello to the extraordinary. Trust us, your competitors won't see it coming. Oh, and you're welcome!

Let's get real. You've got top-notch products/services, but are your followers truly in on the action? They're loving the end result, but have they seen the magic happen? Especially with food. Because let's face it - who isn't a little dubious about what goes on behind the scenes? Cleanliness is king, folks. Your customers might be over the moon with your products, but they're always going to wonder about the how. Show them. Prove it. Give them the backstage pass to your process. Trust us - pull back the curtain and watch those one-time customers turn into die-hard fans. How's that for loyalty?

Let's Get Visual!

Let's address a major Instagram misconception. If you think just slapping pretty pictures on your Instagram page will automatically turn your personal or business brand into an Influencer status symbol, you better think again. You've got to be more than just a pretty face. You need to be a visual virtuoso, a picasso of pixels. You've got a sea of followers out there, thirsting for some eye candy. And it's up to you to give 'em what they want. But remember, it's not just about looking good; it's about making sense too. And more importantly: staying on brand, right?! RIGHT!

Speaking of which, your brand isn't just a logo or a tagline – it's a whole vibe, an experience to be felt, not just seen or heard. So, the visuals you put out there should scream your brand's essence (and presence!), not just be a random assortment of aesthetically pleasing images. Otherwise, your followers might as well be trying to read a book in the dark.

So, go ahead, mix up those colors, play with those filters, but remember – your visuals are your brand's voice in the Instagram choir. Make sure they're singing the right tune, and everything's in sync. Otherwise, it's Buh Buh Bye! to Bossing Up on the 'gram.

Get Smart with Hashtags!

Want to know a trade secret? Hashtags are your new best friend. No need to get all creative. Just jump on the bandwagon of what's already trending. Simply put: use what's hot. Good news - there's always something related to your brand. Why? Because hashtag culture is always booming, baby! We're all so obsessed with them, it's like they've become our new love language.

Every industry, every brand, they're all riding the hashtag wave daily. From Instagram to LinkedIn, it's a hashtag frenzy. So, keep your eyes peeled for those golden hashtag opportunities. Remember, timing is everything. You snooze, you lose.

Why should you care about hashtags? Simple. It's like hitching a ride on a trend train. Social media platforms are like hawks, spotting similar hashtags and bundling them together. It's like a social media matchmaking service, bringing together posts and brands with a shared mission. It's your golden ticket to get your brand in front of more eyeballs. So, leveraging trending hashtags? It's not just a good move, it's the move.

Boss Up Your Instagram Profile

Hate to burst your bubble but there are no shortcuts to Insta-success. Try as you may but sooner or later you'll find out the hard way: have the right system and strategy or just keep on failing. First things first, you gotta make your profile description (aka the Bio) sparkle brighter than a unicorn at a disco party. You see, social media is like a giant game of chess, with each move more calculated than a math nerd's prom proposal.

Fact: not every brand can rock the same strategy. What works for one might be a total flop for another. It's like expecting everyone to look good in neon leggings - not gonna happen, champ. So do your homework, dig deep, and find what makes your brand tick. In other words, find your shtick and stick to it like white on rice!

Now, onto the nitty-gritty. Optimizing (aka Bossing Up) your brand on Instagram isn't just about slapping on a filter and calling it a day. You gotta figure out the sweet spot for your own unique style of pics and reels and stories. It includes tone of voice, writing style, fonts, colors, type of music, word count, it's your Insta-Identity aka how you present your brand to followers on Instagram. It's like dressing for a date - know what works for you. And more crucially, what doesn't.

Bottom line, figure out and craft your brand, do your research, and keep your Insta-game strong. Because nobody ever won the internet by playing it safe. So go on, dive in, and make some waves with your brand on Instagram.

You + Instagram Analytics = BFF

Sure, all these fancy strategies sound great, but how do you know if they're actually worth your time? You gotta measure them, my friend. It's all about that sweet, sweet data. Instagram is no dummy, they've given us some slick tools like Analytics, Curalate and BlitzMetrics to keep an eye on how our brands are doing.

These babies let you track likes and comments on your posts. So, you can see if all those late-night brainstorming sessions and strategic posts are actually bagging you more followers. Not seeing the results? Maybe it's time to switch up your game. Stick with the strategies that are getting you that Instagram love and ditch the ones that are just taking up space. It's all about working smarter, not harder, right?

Capture Your Brand's Pivotal Moments

You've heard the word on the street, right? All the cool kids, or should I say, social media wizards, are raving about the power of bite-sized videos. Yep, you heard that right. Your brand's shiny moments don't need to be full-length documentaries. Keep it short, keep it sweet. And always keep it on brand.

Think about it. What's more likely to grab your audience's attention on Instagram - a 2000-word essay, or a quick, easy-to-digest reel? Exactly. You've got product launches coming up? Snap a preview. Got some hot-off-the-press news? Film it. Want to show off your brand's popularity? Record your fans' love letters to your brand. Now turn those into a carousel of pics (you can upload max 10 in one single post). Or, turn them into a 10-30 secs videoclip, selecting trending audio/music and droppin' a fresh caption that will make followers drop Fire Emoji in the comments section.

Here's the kicker though - it's not just about broadcasting. It's about co-creating. Get your audience in on the action. Let them help shape your brand's story. Show them you're not some faceless corporation, but a brand that listens, engages, and appreciates them.

So, what are you waiting for? Get filming, get sharing, and watch your brand's Insta-presence skyrocket.

Expand Your Brand's Instagram's Horizons

Check it out, here's a secret scoop: scrounging followers from big-shot brands on Instagram? Not a sin, pal. Those old dogs have a sea of followers that you'd love to swim in. Loads of businesses have climbed the Insta ladder by hitching a ride on the follower train of the big-wigs. And guess what? You could be the next success story.

How do you get in on this? Start rubbing virtual shoulders with these related brands. Drop likes and comments on their posts like it's hot. This ain't rocket science. You become part of their crowd, you get noticed by their followers. In short, you get to crash the party and walk away with a bunch of potential followers for your brand. So, why not broaden your Instagram horizon riding on the coattails of established brands? It's not cheating. It's being Insta-Savvy!

Don't Be Boring And Predictable. Stay Fresh Always

Hey Insta-fam, it's time to shake things up! Why keep scrolling through the same old, same old when you can serve up some fresh, juicy content that'll leave your followers begging for more? Picture this: you, the Picasso of posts, crafting content that sparks conversation and raises eyebrows. Take a page from ABC World News' playbook – they've got their followers on their toes with sneak peeks of what's hot off their broadcasting press. Pretty genius, right? Your followers are craving something new and exciting, and who are you to deny them that? So, are you ready to step outside your comfort zone and give your content a much-needed glow up? Trust us, your Instagram game will thank you.

Be Slightly And Carefully Controversial

Playing the controversy card to lure clicks? Not the classiest move, but let's be real, it's a guilty pleasure we all dig. Social media marketers have been milking this for ages. Instagram, Facebook, Twitter, LinkedIn, you name it. They've all been used as stages for scandalous news or juicy gossip to reel in the masses. And guess what? It works like a charm.

However, before you start your gossip column on Instagram, remember, with great power comes great responsibility. You wouldn't want to be known as the drama queen/king of the platform, would you? Sure, a sprinkle of controversy here, a pinch of gossip there, can spice up your Instagram content. But too much of it? That's a recipe for disaster. You don't want your followers to start associating your brand with scandal, do you? Nope!

In short, a little controversy can go a long way in making your Instagram page the talk of the town. Just remember, moderation is key. You wouldn't want your brand to be remembered for the wrong reasons, would you? Of course not.

Don't Hate. Geo-Locate!

Ever wondered why it's crucial to drop that location pin on your Instagram bio? Especially when you're a newbie on Instagram, your followers are curious about where you're posting from. With Instagram's geo-location features, it's a breeze to tag your current city or town when setting up your bio. This helps your followers pinpoint your whereabouts – easy-peasy lemon squeezy!

Being upfront about your location on your bio has its perks. For businesses, it's a game-changer. Your followers can gauge whether they can benefit from your business based on the distance. With the correct location info on your bio, you're more likely to reel in the right crowd who won't just double-tap your posts, but will also shell out their dough for what you're selling. In essence, the right location info ensures you attract followers who are conveniently nearby to splurge on your offerings. Also, it gives you a heads up about your competition in the same market. This knowledge equips you to strategize on how to outshine your rivals.

In the grand scheme of things, the right location info boosts your credibility among your existing and prospective customers. Sure, your marketing game might be on point on Instagram and not necessarily need your location, but your potential followers? They need reassurance that your brand is the real deal. Being honest about your location is one way to establish trust among your followers. It's all about winning their trust, and sharing your location is a step in the right direction. So, why not give it a shot? Include your operation location in your Instagram bio and watch your follower's trust level soar. Who knows, it could be the secret sauce to your brand's success.

The Celebrities Factor

So, you're thinking of riding the coattails of celebs on Instagram to make your brand shine? It's not a new trick, but hey, if it ain't broke, don't fix it, right?

Here's the deal. This ain't just about following big-name brands. Nope. It's about rubbing digital shoulders with the rich and famous, the influencers, the people who've got more followers than a lost puppy in a Disney movie. You follow them, you comment on their posts, you like their photos, and you hope their fans start to notice you.

Sounds simple, right? Well, don't pop the champagne just yet. Getting noticed by these high-flyers is a bit like trying to get served at a crowded bar. You've got to be persistent, you've got to be patient, and you've got to have something they want. You know, like free drinks... or in this case, relevant content.

But keep at it, and eventually, you'll strike gold. After all, even a celeb's got to look around and notice who's been shouting their praises. And when they do, you'll be there, ready to swoop in and steal their adoring fans.

Sounds cunning, right? Well, that's the game, folks. Play it right, and you could be the next big thing on Instagram.

So, you want to win over the hearts of celebs and public figures, huh? Not a bad idea, but it's gonna take a bit more than just liking their posts. Here's the lowdown.

First off, you've got to do your homework. Study their posts like you're cramming for finals. Figure out what makes them tick and what's gonna tick them off. Once you've got the lowdown on their likes and dislikes, you're ready to play your hand. Start sending out those seductive posts that hit all the right notes. If your content catches their eye, there's a good chance they'll hit that follow button. And when that happens, get ready for the floodgates to open – their fans will come rushing to your page like kids to an ice cream truck.

Sounds like a goldmine, right? Well, hold your horses. Just because a celeb's got a million followers doesn't mean they're your ticket to fame. You've got to be smart about it. Only follow celebs who are a good fit for your brand. Don't waste your time on someone just because they're popular. Their style has to jive with what you're selling. Align your brand with the right stars, and you'll see those desired results.

Bottom line? Riding the coattails of celebrities and notable public figures can skyrocket your Instagram game – but only if you do it right. Play it smart, stay persistent, and you just might strike marketing gold.

Your Competition can be a Potential Ally. Say Whaaaat?!

Look, we've all been there—seeing your business competitors as your arch-nemeses. But here's a spicy take: in the Instagram marketing world, your rivals are actually your secret superpower. Hear me out, just because you're both hustling the same gig doesn't mean you should be giving each other the side-eye. Your competitors are your golden ticket to Insta-success.

Why not slide into their DMs for a little friendly team-up? Cross-promotion, baby. It's like a superhero crossover event, but for brands. You scratch their back, they scratch yours, and everybody wins. Sure, it's a bit cozy, but it's also smart. Your Insta visibility skyrockets, your sense of community strengthens, and you both get to share the limelight. Plus, you're killing two birds with one stone—boosting your brand and shaking up the status quo.

So, ready to take your Insta game to the next level? Start by buddying up with the competition and watch your followers multiply.

Teaming up with your rivals to swap posts on Insta? Sounds crazy, right? Yet, it's a smart move for scoring big marketing points. But folks, it's not all sunshine and rainbows. You've got to play this game right.

First off, your buddy brand needs to vibe with you. You're trying to get more eyeballs on your content, right? So you need to be in the same ballpark, selling stuff that's at least a little bit related. You can't team up a sneaker brand with a gourmet cheese shop. It's just weird.

But here's the kicker. What if your Insta partner is a social media rockstar with a gazillion followers, while you're just getting warmed up? That's a raw deal, friend. You're stuck boosting their brand while they barely lift a finger for you. So yeah, this tactic can be a win-win. Or it can be a win-lose. Choose wisely.

Get on the Map!

Alright, let's talk about this little gem called Photo Map. It's like a GPS for your Instagram posts. You take a photo, slap a geo-tag on it, and boom - your followers know exactly where you were when you took that epic sunset shot or that mouth-watering food pic. The cool kids on Facebook have been doing it for a while, and now it's Instagram's turn to join the party.

But hang on a second - did you know that photos with geo-tags get a whopping 80% more engagement than their tag-less counterparts? So, not only does your audience know where you're hanging out, but they're way more likely to give your posts some love. It's like magic, but real.

And here's the kicker - Photo Map isn't just a fun add-on for your travel pics. It's a legit game-changer for businesses. Got a physical location? Show it off. It's like a beacon for your brand, telling your audience, "Hey, we're here and we're legit." And let's face it - who doesn't love a brand that's not afraid to put itself on the map?

But wait, there's a catch. You can't just post pics from your business location all the time. That's like wearing the same outfit every day - it gets old. Fast. So, you gotta mix it up a bit. Post from different locations. Keep 'em guessing. Sure, it might cause a bit of confusion, but hey - life's an adventure, right? Just remember to use those geo-tags wisely, and only when you're at your business location. And if you don't? Well, that's on you, my friend.

Social Proof Your Brand

Think your brand's got game? Prove it. Social proof it! Get your brand's cheerleading squad together. We're talking brand ambassadors, folks. People who'll rave about your brand on their Insta, show off your products to their pals. Nothing screams credibility like a bunch of people shouting your praises from the digital rooftops.

So, how do you turn your customers into your own personal hype squad? Well, you could start by getting them to snap a pic while they're using your product or hanging out at your store. When they plaster those pics all over their Insta, their followers are gonna want in on the action. Boom, instant brand promotion.

But hold up. It's not all sunshine and rainbows. You're letting these people rep your brand, and they're not even on your payroll. They don't own a piece of your business. Who's to say they won't turn on you down the line? It's a risk. But let's be real here, the social proof these brand ambassadors bring to the table? It's worth it.

Do Off-Line Events! (Meaning in the Real World)

Here's a wild idea: why not throw an actual, physical party? Shake up the digital doldrums and get your Instagram followers out from behind their screens. Because let's face it, who doesn't love a good shindig? Make your Insta-fam feel like they're part of your brand's inner circle.

Where should you throw this soiree? Your place of business or some hip joint that'll cater to everyone's vibe. Just remember, these offline fiestas are all about your brand, your products, your services. You're not just throwing a party; you're selling your story. You're getting your brand out there in a way that's less billboard and more backyard BBQ. It's a two-for-one deal: a fun gathering that doubles as a killer promo for your business. Now, who wouldn't want to RSVP to that?

A little tip for all you social media gurus out there: Throw a party, and make sure everyone on your Instagram knows about it. It's basically an easy-peasy way to get your followers to fall madly in love with your brand. But here's the catch, it only really works for the folks who live close by. I mean, who wouldn't want to roll out of bed and right into a cool event, right?

But let's speak the truth here, not everyone's going to hop on a plane just to attend your shindig. It's a bit of a bummer, but hey, that's just how the cookie crumbles. So, this little strategy of yours, it's a hit or miss depending on where your followers are located. In a nutshell, it's a killer plan for your local crowd, but don't hold your breath for the out-of-towners.

That's All Folks!

Instagram, that trendy photo-sharing app you've been glued to, isn't just for showing off your avocado toast. Nope, it's become the playground for marketers and investors looking to peddle their wares. I mean, why not? With the right strategy, you can turn a platform full of cat pics into a brand awareness powerhouse.

So, you're a marketer? Great. You've got a buffet of options on how to use Instagram to your advantage. You could play the geo-tagging game, making your posts location-aware. Or you could fanboy over celebrities, riding their coattails to boost your profile and product. And hey, why not team up with your competitors while you're at it? Because nothing says 'progressive brand' like a bit of healthy competition.

At the end of the day, your brand is as unique as a snowflake in a blizzard. So, it's on you and your marketing gurus to conjure up the perfect Insta-strategy. No pressure, right? You got this!

Now get out there, equipped with all this info, put it in practice, set things into motion. Some tips and secrets will work, others might not or might take time. But at least now you know more or less how to hack that pesky algorithm and **Instagram Like a BOSS!**

About Grow Social Flow

We're Grow Social Flow, the fresh-faced, caffeine-fueled kids on the block, determined to shake up the social media game. Born in the vibrant chaos of May 2024, straight outta Dubai, and we're here to turn your Instagram dreams into reality. Tired of scrolling through endless feeds of mediocrity? Join the club. That's why we're here to rescue you from the algorithm abyss.

We're not your average social media agency. We're your hype squad, your digital cheerleaders, your secret weapon for Instagram domination. Think of us as the personal trainers of your online persona. We'll sculpt your feed, build your brand, and help you flex your digital muscles like a boss.

So, if you're ready to ditch the followers and start building a loyal fan base, let's chat. We've got the tools, the talent, and the thirst for success. After all, who better to guide you through the jungle of Instagram than a couple of wild-eyed social media experts?

Follow us on Insta: @GrowSocialFlow

Check out our other e-books: https://linktr.ee/growsocialflow

Drop us a line: message at: growsocialflow@gmail.com

Instagram Like A Boss!